Original title:
Timber Tales and Tidbits

Copyright © 2025 Creative Arts Management OÜ
All rights reserved.

Author: Henry Beaumont
ISBN HARDBACK: 978-1-80567-191-6
ISBN PAPERBACK: 978-1-80567-490-0

The Natural Narrative

In the woods where squirrels dance,
A raccoon wears a funny pants.
He sneaks a snack, a pie delight,
And giggles loud beneath the night.

The beavers build with sticks and logs,
While frogs debate in ribbit blogs.
A bear with a bow tie sings a tune,
Underneath a smiling moon.

The owls hoot jokes that leave you grinning,
While playful deer engage in spinning.
A rabbit hops with wobbly flair,
Chasing his tail without a care.

With nudged acorns and knotted vines,
These woodland critters draw the lines.
In nature's class of laughter high,
The forest giggles as time flies by.

Tales from the Timber Trails

The squirrels plot a nutty heist,
While chipmunks munch on cheese with zest.
A porcupine tries to breakdance,
With quills that poke, it's quite the chance!

The moose wear sunglasses, style elite,
As they strut down the forest street.
A fox in socks jumps for a treat,
While raccoons tap dance with their feet.

Out by the log, an owl spins yarns,
Of how he once scared off some barns.
The creatures laugh 'til they are sore,
As shadows dance on the forest floor.

In this wild world of giggles bright,
Each critter shares its silly plight.
With every chuckle and every song,
The tales of woods go on and long.

Rhythms of Roots

In the forest where squirrels play,
The acorns dance the night away.
Trees gossip with a rustling sound,
While the odd raccoon spins round and round.

Leaves chuckle as they fall in heaps,
While owls pretend they're counting sheep.
The branches sway to nature's beat,
As critters tap their tiny feet.

Legends of the Leafy Haven

In a glade where shadows dwell,
The mushrooms weave a weary spell.
The foxes hold a secret fair,
While badgers munch on fluffy air.

The trees boast of their height and might,
As beetles race in curious flight.
A chorus hums from frogs so sly,
While butterflies teach chubby ants to fly.

The Banyan's Bounty

Under the shade of gnarled roots,
A picnic's set with leafy fruits.
The monkeys swing, they snatch a fry,
While pigeons just roll by and sigh.

The banyan's arms, so large and stout,
Hide all the snacks without a doubt.
The laughter of the breeze is loud,
As friends enjoy the leafy crowd.

Songs of the Sylvan Sanctuary

In the sanctuary where giggles roam,
The trees become our vibrant home.
The songbirds twirl and twist and dive,
While the crooked branches laugh and jive.

Flowers flash their colors bright,
As ants march past in strict delight.
The sunbeams dance, a playful crew,
While nature's comedy shines anew.

Lush Lore of Leafy Loams

In the forest where squirrels play,
Gossip flies from branch to bay.
The acorns plot their winter feasts,
While chipmunks dance like little beasts.

A tree once claimed it could outgrow,
The tallest pine, with quite a show.
But vines creeped up, quite sly and fast,
Now it's the laughingstock at last.

Each leaf has secrets, whispers loud,
Of bugs that dance and branches bowed.
A beetle once wore a crown so grand,
'Til wind knocked it off, across the land.

So if you stroll through shady glades,
Beware of tricks that nature trades.
For in the woods, the stories thrive,
With giggles from each bush alive!

Myths of the Midwood

Deep in the grove, a legend grew,
Of a raccoon who knew kung fu.
He'd challenge owls to late-night fights,
While hedgehogs claimed they flew like kites.

A wise old owl, with glasses thick,
Said, 'Stop, you fools! You'll break a stick!'
But off they went, all agile and spry,
As rabbits laughed, just passing by.

Mice told tales of a giant cat,
Who snored so loud, it shook the mat.
You'd think the woods would fall asleep,
But squirrels chuckled, "He'll never leap!"

So wander where the acorns roll,
And listen close to the forest's soul.
For every rustle, every caw,
Is a giggle-wrapped, enchanting law.

Grove of Glimmering Tales

In a grove where stories twinkle bright,
A frog donned glasses, a curious sight.
He croaked of adventures far and wide,
While crickets chirped, "Do not bide!"

A snail claimed speed, and oh, what fun!
He raced past shadows, but hardly won.
With a sprint so slow, a joke in tow,
He'd gather foes and steal the show.

The flowers giggled, swaying high,
At passersby, they'd wink and sigh.
For bees wore hats, with fancy flair,
And bumblebees danced, without a care.

So if you hear a giggle near,
It's nature's laughter that draws you here.
Embrace the whimsy, let it roam,
In this patch of joy, you're truly home!

Echoes through the Elders

Once stood a stump, quite proud and bold,
Claimed he had stories, oh, so old.
But moss rolled eyes and whispered soft,
'You're just a seat for birds to loft!'

An elder tree, with bark like age,
Said, 'Hey young saplings, turn the page!'
As children laughed with glee, a play,
A squirrel tossed acorns, hip-hip-hooray!

The hoverflies wore sunglasses cool,
While fireflies shone like jewels in school.
A dance-off started under the moon,
The woods alive, a lively tune.

So raise your voice in the forest bright,
Join the echoes in the fading light.
For every tale that rustles the leaves,
Is a giggle shared among the eaves!

Secrets of the Silvan Sphere

In the woods, a squirrel pranced,
Wore a hat that glimmered, danced.
He claimed to be a forest king,
But all he ruled were acorns' bling.

The rabbit laughed and took a seat,
Said, "Your crown makes you quite the treat!"
But as he hopped and made a mess,
He left behind a leafy dress.

The owl perched high with wise old eyes,
Sipped on tea as if to jest,
"These woods are full of silly schemes,
Like frogs who wear pajamas in dreams."

Now every tree holds secrets tight,
Of critters who just want to bite,
A piece of cake, a loaf of bread,
A funny tale before the bed.

Forest Fables and Folklore

A fox once tried to bake a pie,
With mushrooms scooped from branches high.
But every time he stirred the pot,
Out came a meal that hit the spot!

A deer enrolled in dance ballet,
With hooves that twirled in a fine display.
But tripped on roots, oh such a sight!
She laughed so hard, she sparked delight.

The raccoon thought he'd steal the show,
Yet bumped into a tree, oh no!
With eyes so wide, he danced away,
Swiping snacks without delay.

In this forest full of glee,
Every critter claims they see,
The quirkiest of tales unfurled,
A hidden laugh in nature's world.

Echoes in the Evergreen

A parrot perched with tales to tell,
Of all the squirrels who fell and fell.
"I borrowed this from a hedgehog friend,
Recounting how their antics never end!"

A beaver held a gala grand,
With guests who waddled, shared a band.
But every tune, a splashy flop,
As dancers twirled and bopped and dropped.

The porcupine wore a spike-filled hat,
Declared, "I'm fashionable, how 'bout that?"
Yet every critter turned to stare,
And found his style rather rare.

In echoes bright from trees so tall,
You'll hear the giggles that enthrall.
Life's oddities fill the air,
In every nook and hidden lair.

Pinecone Parables

A pinecone claimed it came from space,
A world where trees could win a race.
Yet every time it lost its grip,
It tumbled down with quite the flip.

A frog in boots leaped high and far,
Said he could jump to touch a star.
But landing funny on a sprig,
He giggled hard, "What a big dig!"

A crow thought wisdom made him sage,
He talked of crumbs and gilded page.
Yet lost his snack, to his dismay,
He cawed aloud, "What's this, fah-lay?"

In this realm of quirky fun,
Each tale unfolds, we've just begun.
With laughter shared among the leaves,
The forest speaks, and joy deceives.

The Enchanted Understory

Beneath the boughs where critters play,
A squirrel sings in a silly way.
He twirls a nut with acrobats,
While chatting with the ponderous cats.

A rabbit hops with crazy grace,
He dreams of winning a dance-off race.
With leaps so grand, he steals the scene,
While chuckling at a cat's cuisine.

A wise old owl, eyes all aglow,
Says, "Life's a joke, enjoy the show!"
With laughter ringing through the trees,
Even the breezes carry glee.

So if you wander through the glade,
Prepare for laughs in the sun and shade.
For squirrels and rabbits hold a grand spree,
In this merry land of joyful glee.

Whimsy of Wandering Roots

Roots twist and turn beneath the ground,
Whispering secrets all around.
They play a game of hide and seek,
Tickling toes of ones who peek.

A wandering beetle, quite bemused,
Dances on roots, feeling enthused.
He spins and twirls upon a breeze,
While chatting up the giggling leaves.

In shadows deep where mischief brews,
A gnome in socks has little shoes.
He juggles acorns with such flair,
Declaring, "Watch me, if you dare!"

So follow where the wild roots roam,
You'll find the laughter feels like home.
In every nook, from ground to bough,
Funny surprises await you now.

Dreams in the Driftwood

Driftwood dreams float on the creek,
Where fish pop up for a little peek.
A turtle parks with a sunhat on,
Claiming this log as his own salon.

The otters slide and giggle loud,
Creating ripples in a crowd.
"Watch us dance!" they squeak and slide,
While laughter rings from side to side.

A bottle cap, a pirate's prize,
Transforms into a treasure size.
"Finders keepers," shout the frogs,
As they hold court with drifting logs.

In this silly world, all dreams take flight,
Where driftwood tales dance in delight.
So cast your worries down the stream,
And join the fun in this dream team!

The Timberland Tapestry

In the patchwork woods of vibrant hues,
Each tree tells tales of playful news.
With knots and twists, they weave a plot,
Of shy deer prancing and jumping a lot.

A mischievous fox, with a grin so wide,
Challenges trees to a friendly slide.
Down barky slopes, they giggle and sway,
As birds chirp tunes of a zany ballet.

A woodpecker drums the beat of fun,
While badgers groove, not wanting to run.
With laughter ringing from root to leaf,
This frolic creates the finest relief.

So stroll through this tapestry of glee,
Where woodland antics are wild and free.
Embrace the charm of mischief's cheer,
For joy in the woods is always near.

The Lore of the Limbs

In the woods where branches sway,
Squirrels plot a nutty play.
A raccoon steals the show each night,
Dancing in the moon's soft light.

Trees gossip about the breeze,
While owls chuckle from the trees.
A fox sneaks in with clever tricks,
The forest hums with nature's kicks.

Beneath the roots, the rabbits laugh,
Playing tag with nature's path.
Each creak and crack of a log, they hear,
A symphony of joy and cheer.

Oh, the tales that bark can tell,
Of secret meetings, what a swell!
In every trunk and mossy nook,
A funny story waits, like a book.

Pine Whispers and Willow Whimsy

By the river, willows sway,
Whispering secrets of the day.
A playful splash, a frog leaps high,
While birds tease clouds in the sky.

Pines giggle under summer's sun,
Sharing jokes until the day is done.
A squirrel scolds a tree for shade,
In this dance, no fun is made.

Branches stretch for a game of toss,
Bouncing acorns, what a loss!
Laughter echoes through the glade,
Nature's charm, forever displayed.

So when you wander through the green,
Remember the fun that can be seen.
In every leaf and playful breeze,
Life's a merry, leafy tease.

Canopied Confessions

Underneath the leafy shade,
Secret confessions are relayed.
The chipmunk shares a nutty tale,
Of a bird that sings like a whale.

A badger winks, says 'Let's not tell,'
As crickets chirp their little spell.
Twinkling stars come out to play,
While fireflies dance, leading the way.

In canopies of leafy dreams,
The forest weaves its funny schemes.
A deer prances, trying to glide,
With a clumsy leap, it takes a ride.

So gather 'round the trunks so wide,
And join the laughter, let it slide.
For in this haven of trees and light,
The confessions bloom, oh what a sight!

Rustic Reveries

In a glen where wildflowers grow,
A snail tells tales that tickle slow.
About the time he raced a hare,
And lost his shell without a care.

Old logs hold laughter over the years,
Echoing soft, the woodsy cheers.
Where critters gather, don't be shy,
You might hear a punchline fly.

The sunbeam tickles each twig and leaf,
Turning every simple moment, a thief.
Chasing shadows, the laughter unfolds,
In rustic memories, much fun it holds.

So when you wander, take a break,
Join the dance, for goodness' sake.
In nature's arms, the joy is clear,
Rustic reveries, bring us near.

Bark-bound Ballads

In the forest, the squirrels convene,
They discuss pinecones, if you know what I mean.
With acorns as currency, they barter away,
And laugh at the leaves that just drift and sway.

A woodpecker poses with immense pride,
Knocking on trees like a rhythmic guide.
He claims he can tell the age of each bough,
But all of us know, he has no clue how!

The rabbits in coats made of leafy attire,
Hold fashion shows that inspire no fire.
They prance and they twirl, in a dandelion breeze,
Yet trip on their tails, oh, dear, what a tease!

As the sun sets low, the tales grow tall,
Of epic adventures in shadows that sprawl.
With giggles and cheers, under moonlit skies,
Nature's own laughter is a grand surprise!

Wisdom Woven in Wood

The sage old tree with a wise old face,
Hands down advice in a slow, steady pace.
"Don't lose your bark in the wind and rain,
Embrace who you are, for it's never in vain!"

The chipmunks chattered, oh what a debate,
Arguing fiercely over snacks on their plate.
"If wisdom is nuts, then I surely must be,
The smartest around—don't you see my glee?"

A tale of the owl, revered and profound,
Who hooted at wisdom very loudly around.
"Life's just like branches, they twist and they bend,
But forge your own path; do not just pretend!"

And as twilight glows, the creatures all say,
"Our forest is quirky in its funny way.
With laughter and joy, take each day in stride,
For living in nature is truly our pride!"

Odes to the Old Oak

Oh, majestic oak with your branches spread wide,
You've seen all the seasons, in you we confide.
With squirrels who nest in your mighty embrace,
Whenever they laugh, it's a real happy place.

You creak and you groan, but you stand ever tall,
While the mischievous wind plays tag with your call.
With leaves that wag fingers, they tease and they jest,
"Find shelter with us, your heart shall find rest!"

The time you once witnessed a raccoon's great heist,
When they stole all the snacks—oh, what a wild feast!
With owlish disputes that would keep you awake,
Life under your branches is never a mistake.

So here's to you, oak, with your stories untold,
In rings of your trunk, many moments unfold.
To nature's grand laughter and joy we shall cheer,
For you are a legend who brings us great cheer!

The Heartbeat of the Hollow

In the heart of the hollow, where stories abound,
The critters convene with their giggles and sound.
With tales of the badger who stole all the cheese,
They roll on the grass with the greatest of ease.

The fireflies flicker, a most dazzling show,
While the frogs croak their legends, both fast and slow.
And whispers of gossip float up to the moon,
As owls hoot along, setting nature's grand tune.

In the dusk of the evening, the laughter takes flight,
As mischief unfolds in the soft, starry night.
With shadows that dance and the branches that sway,
The heartbeat of hollow brings joy to our play.

So gather, dear friends, in the warmth of this light,
Where the moon spills its secrets into the night.
In this quirky old hollow, where spirits do play,
We celebrate life in the funniest way!

Evergreen Eulogies

In a forest filled with glee,
The pines have quite the spree.
They whisper secrets with delight,
Claiming squirrels plot all night.

A cedar once wore a hat,
Said it made him quite the brat.
But when the breeze gave a huff,
His fancy look was just too tough.

The oaks play cards with the breeze,
Challenging each other with ease.
But dodging acorns in the rush,
Ends the game with quite the crush.

Every tree has tales so tall,
Of woodland dances, a funny ball.
Rooted in laughter, they bend and sway,
In a world of wood, they dance and play.

Beneath the Boughs

Beneath the boughs, a rabbit cheered,
A wobbly squirrel, always revered.
With acorns dressed like fancy jewels,
They sparkle bright, those little fools.

A wise old owl, he starts to snore,
While raccoons plot a munching score.
They've raided the stash of the grumpy duck,
Who now shouts, 'This just isn't luck!'

The mushrooms giggle under their caps,
As chipmunks tumble in playful laps.
Every fungus holds a secret so bright,
In this goofy woodland, we share delight.

Nature's jesters, in the dance of life,
Bringing joy to sweet woodland strife.
With laughter echoing through the night,
Beneath the boughs, all's pure delight.

Shadows of the Canopy

Shadows laugh as leaves do play,
In the sun's warm, cheeky ray.
Branches swing with goofy grace,
Holding secrets in their embrace.

A funky fungus with stripes of gold,
Tells big stories, daring and bold.
With limbs that twist and trunks that cheer,
Every whisper brings more hilarity near.

The beetles sport their shiny coats,
Debating whose fashion truly floats.
As leaf piles become acrobats,
Their flip-flops echo through the spats.

In a world where shadows jest and tease,
The spirits twirl with the whispering breeze.
Nature smiles, with a giggle or two,
In the canopy's grasp, all feels brand new.

The Old Growth's Confessions

Old growth speaks with a creaky tone,
Claiming wisdom, though mostly alone.
'I've seen all things from bumblebees,
To wayward squirrels stealing my leaves.'

Once a branch had a fling with the sun,
But misjudged the timing and missed the fun.
'This bark's no shield, I'm wise to the jest,
And these knots in my trunk? They're just my best.'

A hickory brags of a nutty prize,
While the birch rolls its eyes, 'Oh, really, wise guy?'
The willows just sigh, with a droopy frown,
'We're all just crazy, can't keep us down.'

In the wisdom of laughter lies their creed,
Swaying gently, they plant each seed.
With a chuckle, the old woods still thrive,
In a world where the witty stay alive.

The Life of Twigs and Roots

Twigs often ponder their destiny,
Hoping one day to grow a tree.
Roots gossip deep in the earth,
Wondering which twig had the best birth.

Squirrels stop by for snacks and jokes,
Sharing tales from old oak folks.
While worms wiggle with glee underground,
Plotting their next wild wormy round.

Sunlight tickles leaves' funny faces,
As branches dance in playful races.
And little bugs shoot for the grass,
Hoping their wings will soon amass.

So heed the call of daily blooms,
For laughter in the forest looms.
With every shuffle and sneaky glance,
Nature's joke has its own dance.

Canopy Chronicles

Up above, the branches jest,
Comparing who's growing the best.
A parrot critiques a crow's loud caw,
And vines chatter—'There's no law!'

The sunbeams peek through leafy veils,
Tickling trunks with playful tales.
While a chipmunk on a branch does glide,
He's secretly planning a berry slide.

Bees buzz loudly with all their might,
Declaring themselves the dance-off knight.
Bumblebees wear crowns made of clover,
While flower petals cheer, "Move over!"

Even the shadows have their fun,
Flickering as they play and run.
In the heights where the laughter soars,
Every rustle opens new doors.

Rustic Revelations

Old logs gather round for a tale,
Each groove and knot has a story to unveil.
One shared of a squirrel so bold,
He thought he could steal nuts made of gold.

The whispers of bark fill the air,
As curious critters stop and stare.
"Did you hear about that cheeky crow?"
"Who took a nap and forgot to toe?"

From owls who hoot in the dead of night,
To raccoons who dream of a berry bite—
The stories echo through the woods,
A patchwork of funny ancient goods.

Around the campfire, the wisdom flows,
With laughter sprouting like wildflower shows.
Nature's humor is keen and bright,
Revealing laughs in every light.

Sapling Stories

Young saplings shake off morning dew,
With leaves that giggle at skies so blue.
They dream of stretching towards the sun,
While insect friends join in for fun.

"Is that a squirrel jiving on my toes?"
"Or just a leaf that's tickled by the nose?"
Little roots stake their claim in the ground,
Wiggling with joy at every sound.

The smallest seed who aims to grow tall,
Invents a dance that wobbles for all.
"Watch my dance! Isn't it neat?"
They laugh and sway on their tiny feet.

A breeze brushes past with a giggling tone,
As saplings sway and feel less alone.
In this merry circle of life and light,
The joy of growing feels so right.

The Language of Leaves

Whispers float on gentle breeze,
Leaves gossip tales, if you please.
Acorns roll, squirrels in tow,
They trade secrets; oh, how they go!

Maple laughs at oak's bad hair,
Birch sways, claiming it doesn't care.
Pine needles snicker at the ground,
While wildflowers dance, joy unbound.

Stories Sown in Soil

In the earth, where stories creep,
Worms plot mischief while roots sleep.
Roses sigh of fights with weeds,
And daisies giggle at their needs.

Nutty squirrels hide their stash,
While plants gossip in a dash.
Carrots chuckle, buried so deep,
With tales of dreams, they dare to leap.

Mossy Memories Unraveled

Moss collects whispers from the past,
Tiny tales that grew so vast.
Toadstools chime in, all aglow,
As they share tales of rain and snow.

Old stones grin with lichen's face,
Reminiscing in their cozy space.
Fungi dance with a fungal flair,
Each memory playful, light as air.

Beneath the Bark: A Saga

Underneath where bark hugs tight,
Woodpeckers drum with pure delight.
Tales of growth, both long and tall,
Of storms and laughter coming to call.

Beetles race on a winding track,
While grubs sing songs we can't hold back.
All beneath the sturdy skin,
Is a comical world where life begins.

Secrets of the Silent Grove

In a hollow tree, a squirrel found,
A stash of acorns, snug and round.
He giggled loud, his secret shared,
With birds and fox, all unprepared.

The wise old owl, in her tall perch,
Said, "Don't be loud, it's time for church!"
But the trees shook, with laughter's glee,
As critters danced wild and free.

A raccoon sneaked, with his crafty paw,
To chow on nuts, while breaking law.
He wore a mask, an outlaw's pride,
In the quiet grove, he couldn't hide.

So if you wander, just beware,
Secrets linger in the fresh, cool air.
In every nook, a tale to tell,
Of nature's laughs, all's merry and well.

Bark and Bristle

A porcupine, with prickly flair,
Wore a bark hat, a stylish air.
He strutted deep with spiky pride,
While the dandelions giggled by his side.

The beavers laughed from their hefty dam,
"Look at that hat! He's such a sham!"
With a splash of water and a wink,
They tossed him twigs, and started to think.

A squirrel proposed a wacky craze,
"Let's have a contest in funny ways!"
With branches twined and laughter bright,
They crowned the porcupine king that night.

So join the fun, if you dare,
In the woodland fashionista's lair.
Where every creature picks a style,
And the prickle-and-peck brings out a smile.

A Symphony of Stumps

In the meadow where stumps abound,
The critters gathered round, astound.
With drumsticks made from fallen limbs,
They played a tune, as nature hymns.

A fox on flute, quite out of tune,
Howled like the wind, beneath the moon.
The rabbits thumped, a percussive beat,
While turtles grooved on their tiny feet.

A badger danced, with lumbering grace,
Bumping the hedgehog into space.
With twirling tails and snickers fine,
They all agreed, it was divine!

So if you find a stump in sight,
Join the symphony, dance with delight.
For in that grove, where laughter reigns,
Music is found in friendship's chains.

The Wind's Wooden Stories

The wind whispered secrets through the leaves,
Of giggling squirrels and mischievous thieves.
A tale of a log that rolled away,
Bringing laughter to a bright, sunlit day.

Through towering spruces, the breezes blow,
Tickling the branches with tales they know.
Of fairies who danced on twigs up high,
And visions of fish that hopped in the sky.

A wise old cedar swayed with glee,
Telling of moments where all felt free.
From acorns falling to owls' deep hoots,
The wind's wooden stories give timeless roots.

So listen closely, as breezes weave,
Wooden tales that make hearts believe.
In every gust, a chuckle sings,
Of laughter born on natural wings.

Roots of Remembrance

In a forest so tall, where squirrels conspire,
Old roots whisper stories, never to tire.
A wise old tree grumbles, 'Watch where you tread!'
'You step on my toes, and I'll knock off your head!'

Beneath leafy covers, the mushrooms all chatter,
'Keep it down, will you? We're not here to flatter!'
The rabbits just giggle, with cheeks full of greens,
While the owls roll their eyes, and plot silly schemes.

A bumblebee buzzes, with swagger so grand,
"I'm the best pollinator across this whole land!"
But the flies just roll over, they scoff and they snicker,
'Last Monday you tripped on your own little ticker!'

As night softly falls, they all gather near,
With fireflies dancing, they sing without fear.
Laughs echo through trunks, in this wild, wacky place,
For roots worth remembering are filled with grace.

Chronicles of the Canopy

Up high in the boughs, where the critters convene,
A parrot tells tales, with a voice sharp and keen.
'Once I spotted a fox, with a hat far too big!'
And the crowd busts out laughing, led by a twig.

A raccoon leads dances, with moves so absurd,
Swinging and swirling with not one spoken word.
The skunks start to scent, and the squirrels they cheer,
It's a whiff and a giggle, as they twirl all year!

The owls throw a party, with hoots on the side,
They dance through the branches, on the evening tide.
A mockingbird chirps, mixing tunes left and right,
While the woodpecker drums, keeping all spirits bright.

So if you wander up, to the canopy high,
Listen close to the giggles, and faint chuckled sighs.
The chronicles of laughter are tales that won't fade,
In the sun-dappled laughter, wild memories are made.

Sagas of the Sturdy

Sturdy barks echo, as the wind tells a tale,
Of trees that were heroes, never known to fail.
A giant oak bragged, 'I'm the best of the rest!'
While the willows just snickered, 'You're just kind of blessed!'

A pine tree protested, 'I'm tall, sleek, and green!'
But a gnarled old cedar just laughed, 'You're a teen!'
With branches like arms, they all jump and run,
As the laughter cascades, beneath bright golden sun.

The saplings looked on, with eyes full of dreams,
Thinking of big tales and epic schemes.
'One day we'll stand strong, in the sun's warm embrace,'
Surface stories will bloom, in this leafy place!

So gather 'round, friends, for the sagas abound,
Of sturdy old stories, hilarious sounds.
In the hollows of laughter, where the tall tales go,
The woodlands sing softly, with a magical glow.

Legends in the Lichen

In the shadows of bark, where the dampness can cling,
The lichen shares legends of a most foolish king.
'The one that believed, he could jump over logs!'
Now he's known as the jester, with jokes for the frogs.

A snail in a shell spins a yarn made of slime,
Of races with turtles, his not-so-fast time.
A mole in the dark, with secrets to share,
Claps his little paws, filled with laughter and air.

Old boulders chuckle, as the dew drops all fall,
They tell of a squirrel that once tried to be tall.
He slipped on a leaf, and he tumbled away,
Now he's the town hero, the jester they'll say!

The legends emerge, from the earth and the stone,
Of creatures and antics in a world all their own.
With humor so light, like the air all aglow,
The lichen beams proudly, as their stories grow.

Splinters of Memory

In the woods where the squirrels play,
A raccoon tried to dance all day.
He slipped on a log, what a sight!
Laughed by the moon, it was quite the night.

The tree trunk whispered, 'Don't be a fool!'
'That dance move belongs to the pool.'
A bird chirped a fit, lost in laughter,
While branches swayed, seeking a partner.

Among the roots, a frog did croak,
A legend once told of a leaping bloke.
He jumped so high, kissed the sky,
But fell for a twig; oh my, oh my!

So next time you wander where trees grow tall,
Remember the creatures, don't let them fall.
For every leaf tells a story, it's true,
With giggles and splinters, they welcome you.

Nature's Narrative

The owls gather round, a scholarly bunch,
With wise old tales, they munch and crunch.
They hoot like it's news from long ago,
While the rabbits just roll, stealing the show.

The bushes gossip with rustling leaves,
'Have you seen that fox? What tricks he weaves!'
They chuckle and sway, with whispers so light,
While the flowers giggle at the silly night.

A lumberjack's axe, with a nickname so grand,
'Choppy McChopface,' he rules the land.
He swings with glee, a comedic fright,
Accidentally chopped a gnome's hat in spite.

But nature, it knows how to have some fun,
From fawns who prance in the warm sun.
Each creature's a player in this woodland spree,
With humor and antics surrounding the trees.

Forested Folktales

Once lived a bear, named Benny the Bold,
Who thought he could dance, or so he was told.
He twirled on the grass, but stumbled to fall,
Now, his friends call him Benny the Wall.

The raccoon brought snacks to the woodland show,
But the snacks were all stolen by a sneaky doe.
She giggled and pranced, with snacks in her mouth,
While Benny just glared, feeling quite south.

A parade of the critters, quite merry and bright,
With ants on parade, marching left and right.
Their tiny ant hats were a laugh to behold,
As they pranced with pride, so brave and so bold.

When twilight descends, the owls start their tune,
Singing of antics beneath the big moon.
For every tree trunk holds a giggling glee,
In a world full of mirth, wild and free.

Serene Stories in Sap

In the stillness of woods, the tales take flight,
With a chipmunk named Charlie, a real delight.
He stashed all his acorns, quite a clever chap,
But forgot where he hid them, oh what a trap!

A partridge once claimed he could soar through the air,
Until he met branches, and fluffed up his hair.
Now he struts around, with a feathery flair,
Just a ground-bound prince with no need for a pair.

Every pine tree chuckles with its sap so sweet,
While stories unfold at each winding retreat.
The wind carries whispers, a giggling breeze,
As critters convene, sharing secrets with ease.

So listen closely as dusk does approach,
For nature's own laughter is here to encroach.
In every tick-tock of the forest's own map,
Lie serene little stories, sweet as the sap.

Enchanted Boughs

In the forest where squirrels prance,
A tree once wore pants by chance.
It strutted and danced, a sight so grand,
But tripped on its roots, oh how it spanned!

The birds in hats would cheer and clap,
While raccoons giggled, taking a nap.
They claimed the tree was quite the star,
With branches that strummed a guitar!

Each evening a party would start,
With fireflies flickering, a work of art.
The sap dripped like honey, sweet and fun,
And knotted wood always made a pun.

So next time you wander under those bows,
Remember their quirks, their giggles, their vows.
For in every ole branch, a mystery lingers,
A slice of laughter captured in fingers.

The Poetry of the Pines

Under the pines, where shadows play,
The squirrels compose a ballet every day.
They twirl and leap with nuts as their props,
While owls look on, giving wise head nods.

A pine cone debated a tree on style,
Claiming with pride, 'I make folks smile!'
But the bark just chuckled, 'You're just a nut,
I've got rings of wisdom, now let's strut.'

A gust of wind joins in on the fun,
Sending hats flying, not one's safe run.
The forest erupted in laughter once more,
As the pines swayed, a leafy uproar.

If you listen closely, you might just hear,
The whisper of joy, ringing loud and clear.
In a world made of laughter, with moments divine,
The poetry flows from the heart of the pines.

Whispers of the Wildwood

In the wildwood, shadows bring cheer,
Where leaves gossip softly, oh so near.
A fox tells jokes, quite the comedian,
While deer roll their eyes, it's a wild medium!

Rabbits with giggles hop down the lane,
Chasing their tails, oh what a game!
The trees hold their breath, fearing a laugh,
For a chuckle here could cause a big gaffe.

A bashful raccoon with pie on its face,
Wonders if this is his rightful place.
But the owls just hoot, and the badgers all cheer,
Each moment a treasure, every story sincere.

So wander, dear friend, through this delightful maze,
Where laughter is interwoven in the sun's warm rays.
For in every whisper, a giggle resides,
In the wildwood magic where joy never hides.

Tales of the Timberline

At the timberline with humor abound,
Where the trees tell stories, and laughter is found.
A grumpy old tree bragged of its age,
While a young sprout giggled, 'You're just a stage!'

The breeze told tales of ribbons and bows,
Of woodland dances and curious crows.
The mountain's echoes amplified cheer,
As critters shared legends with everyone near.

One day a raccoon stole a hat on a dare,
And the badgers rolled over, unable to bear!
With every mishap, a lesson bestowed,
In the tapestry woven where laughter flowed.

So take off your troubles, hang them on a hook,
And join in the stories with every nook.
For at the timberline, where humor's in sight,
Every moment is brighter, every giggle ignites.

Whispers of the Woodland

In the leafy crown, a squirrel pranced,
Chasing shadows, oh how it danced!
A twig snapped loud, he jumped so high,
Thought it was thunder, now watch him fly!

Rabbits giggle, they know the score,
Wagering snacks, who'll reach the door?
With floppy ears, they leap and bound,
In this silly race, there's fun to be found!

A wise old owl, with eyes so round,
Cackles at both from high in her mound.
"Careful now, or you'll spill the tea,
Nature's comedy is wild and free!"

The trees all croon, their branches sway,
Sharing secrets in a chuckling way.
Beneath the sun, they giggle loud,
In this woodland space, joy is found!

Echoes in the Forest

A crow caws out, a joke on his beak,
Telling the leaves, "Hey, I'm not a sneak!"
With ruffled feathers, they laugh so hard,
"Guess who's clumsy? That slippery bard!"

Bambis stroll, with spots so bright,
Strutting their stuff, a delightful sight.
But tripping over shadows, oh what a scene,
They giggle together, the forest's routine!

A fox in a hat, who wears a grin,
Invites all creatures to join in the din.
"Let's throw a party, oh doesn't it gleam?
With acorns and giggles, we'll live the dream!"

The night draws close, the stars peek out,
Creatures all whisper, they dance and shout.
In the echoes of laughter, they revel and play,
In this cozy forest, let's swoon the day!

The Chronicles of Oak and Pine

Once sat an oak with stories ample,
Telling a tale of a pine so dappled.
"Once I got stuck with a hive of bees,
But they loved my shade, just swayed in the breeze!"

The pine chuckled back, "Oh, do tell more!
I once lost a branch in a wind so sore!"
And all the critters gathered around,
Laughing so loud, with joy they abound.

A ladybug chimed in, so petite,
"Dear oak, dear pine, oh what a feat!
You're legends of laughter, in foliage grand,
Each twist and each turn, make life so planned!"

Their tales intertwined in giggles and glee,
Creating a saga as light as the breeze.
In the heart of the woods, they'd whisper and jest,
In this merry realm, we're truly blessed!

Snippets from the Canopy

High in the branches, the parakeets chat,
Gossiping gaily while munching on fat.
"Who wore that nest? It's quite the sight!"
They harmonize laughter, pure delight!

A sloth hangs low, in a hammock of vines,
Saying, "Hurry up! Why the long lines?"
While ants promote their speedy parade,
In a race that's slow, watch how they wade!

The sun peeks through, a spotlight of fun,
Every critter here loves to run.
"Catch me if you can!" a jaybird sings,
Fluttering freely, oh how joy clings!

So here in the canopy, life's a hoot,
With laughter and cheer, it's utterly cute.
In the wild and the green, such mischief is grand,
Our secrets of joy, forever will stand!

Echoing Through the Evergreen

In the woods where echoes play,
A squirrel danced in bright array.
He tripped on roots and lost his nut,
Too busy showing off his butt!

A parrot laughed from high above,
He squawked and cawed, a chirpy dove.
The deer just chuckled, shook their heads,
While rabbits giggled in their beds.

A raccoon tried to join the fun,
With a high-pitched squeak, he came undone.
He slipped on leaves, a clumsy feat,
Fell in a puddle, now what a treat!

So under branches, life unfolds,
With laughter shared in stories bold.
A woodland comic, what a sight,
Echoes of joy in morning light.

Barking Up the Right Tree

A dog sat proudly by a tree,
He thought it was the place to be.
He barked like mad at passing cats,
While squirrels rolled their eyes at that.

The tree just stood, not taking sides,
It wore a grin, despite the bides.
A woodpecker, with all his might,
Joined in the barking, what a sight!

The rabbits peeked from leafy shade,
And wondered why the fuss was made.
The dog was sure he ruled this space,
Yet lost a chase and fell from grace!

With barks and laughs that filled the air,
The forest found its own affair.
In furry fun and silly play,
They turned a tree into ballet!

Fables of Fir and Cedar

A fir tree told a tale of old,
Of sneaky foxes, brave and bold.
He swayed and creaked with each delight,
As critters gathered, eyes so bright.

A cedar chimed in with flair,
He spun a yarn of forest wear.
With shoes of bark and hats of leaves,
The animals cheered with laughter's heaves.

The owl found wisdom in their pranks,
As rabbits danced, giving their thanks.
A toad croaked jokes, and frogs all sang,
Until the woods with laughter rang!

As night fell soft, they all agreed,
These stories serve a funny need.
In every twist and turn, they find,
Life's most joyful tales unwind.

Heartbeats in the Hollow

In the hollow where the shadows meet,
A mouse wore shoes made from beet.
He pranced around, pausing to gloat,
While mockingbirds sang, 'You look like a goat!'

A rabbit nearby lost his hat,
Chasing it straight towards a cat.
With leaps and bounds, he ran away,
While the cat just yawned, 'Not today!'

The hedgehog chuckled, spikes in tow,
'These heartbeats echo, don't you know?'
A gathering of giggles filled the air,
With every fumble, joy to share!

So in the hollow, laughter swirled,
As critters danced and flags unfurled.
Their heartbeats synced, a merry chime,
In nature's song, they found their rhyme.

The Singularity of Seeds

Once a tiny seed sat proud,
Dreaming of a sky so loud.
It wished for wings, to take a flight,
But sprouted roots instead—oh, fright!

Said to the sun, "Please give me cheer!"
"I'll dance in soil, my mission clear!"
But every time it tried to sway,
A hungry worm would pull away.

One sprout sighed, "I want some fame!"
"They'll write my story, learn my name!"
Yet all the birds that flew on by,
Just looked and chirped a crazy cry.

In leafy laughter, they convened,
The seeds and worms, a joyful scene.
Together they made quite a fuss,
A playful world, just seeds and dust!

Woven Wood Whimsies

In a forest knot, a squirrel twirled,
With acorns flung, his chaos unfurled.
He crafted hats from leaves galore,
While giggling at the deer who swore.

"I'm the fanciest critter around!"
He chattered loudly, all proud and crowned.
But slipped on bark, with a splat and a thump,
He rolled down a hill, a tumbly lump.

The wise old owl began to hoot,
"Dear squirrel, you must mind your loot!"
But the squirrel just laughed, all out of breath,
Saying, "Life's a gamble, I'll risk it till death!"

Then gathered his friends with a raucous cheer,
For every mishap brought them near.
In the woods, they danced with glee,
A whirlwind of joy—just wild and free!

Bark-bound Epics

In the heart of a tree, a story was spun,
Of a beetle who fancied himself quite the fun.
He bugged every branch, claimed the wood was his,
While the woodpecker laughed with a raucous fizz.

"I'll write a tale from tip to base!"
Said the beetle with dreams to embrace.
But each time he scribbled, a raindrop would fall,
And smudged every letter, no words left at all.

A squirrel swung by, brushing past the trunk,
With a sideways glance at the beetle's funk.
"Why not make songs instead of prose?
Dance to the rhythm as the forest flows!"

So they teamed up to sing, a curious riff,
The bark danced alive, with each happy whiff.
Their stories grew broader, from root up to crown,
In laughter and music, they spread all around!

Cypress Serenades

By the cypress pond, a frog took the stage,
Singing odes to the stars, in his leafy cage.
He croaked out tunes with a twist and a flip,
Making dragonflies giggle, in an air-bound trip.

A fish jumped up, with a splashy remark,
"Your singing's quite bold, but lacks a spark!"
So the frog stuck out his froggy tongue,
And asked the fish to join, in a duet sung.

Together they leaped, a spectacle grand,
Creating a rhythm only nature could understand.
The reeds swayed along, to their jolly spree,
While crickets crooned back, "Oh, sing for us, please!"

In the warm night air, they formed a brigade,
Each note a reminder of the friendships made.
With frogs, fish, and crickets, a marvelous blend,
Echoed through the cypress, a song without end!

The Echoing Grove

In the grove where echo flies,
Trees hold secrets, dressed in sighs.
A squirrel shouts, 'Catch me if you can!'
The owl hoots back, 'Don't be a fan!'

The bushes chuckle, tickled with glee,
As rabbits bicker, 'You can't catch me!'
A deer trips over a log with a thud,
And the forest bursts into laughter and mud.

The sun sets low, casting shadows so long,
The wind whispers jokes, a gentle song.
The leaves join in, rustling their cheer,
In this sly retreat, there's nothing to fear!

As night draws near, with a flicker and glow,
A raccoon declares, 'Let the party flow!'
So gather 'round, creatures both big and small,
In the echoing grove, there's laughter for all!

Narrative in the Nesting Birds

In the branches, tales are spun,
Birds gossip loudly, oh what fun!
A magpie brags, 'I've got the best nest!'
While sparrows chirp, 'Our snooze must be blessed!'

A woodpecker knocks, with a rhythmic beat,
Claiming the title of 'fastest on feet.'
The finches giggle at his hasty claim,
And soon all the birds are joined in the game!

'What's the best worm?' asks the cheeky wren,
'Is it juicy, or just a friend?'
The doves coo softly, sipping their tea,
'Join us again, it's quite the spree!'

As daylight fades, the fun will not cease,
With moonlight's glow, there comes sweet peace.
In the nesting realm where stories are told,
Feathers and laughter make us feel bold!

Sylvan Secrets

In the heart of the woods, there's mischief afoot,
A fox wears a crown, with a clever look!
He declares, 'Today, I'm the king of this den!'
While the rabbits roll eyes, 'Here we go again!'

A badger pipes up, 'Let's start a parade!'
With acorns and leaves, a grand charade.
The chipmunks dance, all hopped up with glee,
While the owls just hoot, sipping their tea!

With every prance and every small cheer,
The trees sway softly, caught up in the sphere.
A raccoon joins in, drums made of bark,
Creating a rhythm that lights up the dark.

As night arrives, the fireflies blink,
Illuminating the fun, more than you'd think.
So come take a seat, on the soft mossy bed,
In this sylvan retreat, join the tales we've bred!

Gnarled Graphs of Time

The old oak stands with a twist and a turn,
It chuckles at time, in its wisdom we learn.
A knot on its trunk says, 'Take a good look!'
While ants march in line, an industrious book.

Lizards sunbathe, claiming prime spots,
Grinning and gossiping, tying up knots.
While shadows stretch long, playing hide-and-seek,
The forest's a stage, it's drama we speak!

A hedgehog strolls with a swagger so proud,
As the wind wraps around like an invisible shroud.
Leaves tumble down, in a whimsical dance,
Leading the critters toward evening's romance.

The moon's hasty ascent invites all to stay,
With laughter and tales, night blooms in array.
In gnarled graphs of time, each moment a rhyme,
Forest frolics abound, in our quirky prime!

Beneath the Bark

Underneath the bark, a squirrel did plan,
To launch a business, a nut-selling man.
He wore a tiny suit, and a tie so neat,
Selling acorns and peanuts, a nutty feat!

His rival, the owl, with glasses so round,
Said, "You'll never win, I'm the smartest around!"
But the squirrel just laughed, with a wink and a twirl,
And said, "Watch my sales fly, give it a whirl!"

With each sales pitch made, the acorns flew fast,
While the owl just hooted, "This will never last!"
But who knew that critters had wallets so fat,
Investing in nuts was the new style, how 'bout that?

And so, in the woods, they call him a champ,
The squirrel with a tie, a real nutty stamp.
But the owl just sighs, with a book on the side,
Reading up on squirrel affairs, what a ride!

Leafy Legends

In the canopy high, where the leaves love to play,
A frog started rapping, much to the trees' dismay.
They whispered and rustled, but he had a groove,
Jamming with insects, who danced to the move!

A beetle beat-boxed, making rhythms so fine,
While the leaves shook their heads, in greenie design.
A tale of a frog, who could bust a great rhyme,
While others just blushed, letting him have his time!

Then a wise old bat joined in on the fun,
Saying, "In this party, everyone's won!"
They laughed 'til they cried, 'neath the moon's silvery sheen,
And songs turned to legends, in this leafy cuisine.

Each night they gather, for more witty banter,
Frog with the fame, and the beetle, the dancer.
Who knew the woods could be so wild and bright,
When legends are made under stars of the night?

Verdant Voices

In a meadow so lush, where the grass likes to sway,
The flowers hold meetings, to gossip and play.
"Did you hear about Daisy? She's blooming quite bold,
And Rose lost her petals, or so I've been told!"

They chattered and chuckled, with laughter in rings,
Discussing the latest in bee-related flings.
The daisies exclaimed, "We heard from the rose,
That bees are just buzzing because of the pose!"

Then Clover chimed in, with a twist of her stem,
"I think it's the honey that lures them to them!"
And the petals all gasped, with a colorful cheer,
Sharing secrets of nature with joy, not a fear!

So in fields of green, where the flowers all sing,
The voices of joy come alive in the spring.
And if you walk by, you might just hear a tale,
Of petals and pollen, on a flowery trail!

Stories in the Sap

In a maple tree trunk lived a story so sweet,
With sap drips and giggles, a sugary treat.
A raccoon once pulled a prank on a bee,
For a pot of that honey, he'd pay to be free!

The bee buzzed in fury, "That's not how it works!
You'll join in the mess, with your nutty quirks!"
So off they both went, to concoct a grand scheme,
To turn the sweet sap into a sticky dream.

They invited the woods, with a sign made of bark,
"Come taste our creation, it's sweet, it's a lark!"
And when all arrived, it was chaos and cheer,
Dancing in mud with the sap-laden beer!

Now in legends they live, those two merry jesters,
Maple sap parties, where nature's investors.
And if you be quiet, 'neath the tall timbered chap,
You might hear their laughter—those stories in sap!

The Whispering Woods: Anecdotes

In the woods, trees gossip loud,
Squirrels wear acorns like a crown.
A deer sneezed, what a hoot!
The red fox laughed, danced about!

Mushrooms giggle, sharing sprees,
Barking trees entice the breeze.
A woodpecker's knock, a jolly sound,
As critters frolic all around!

A wild boar tripped on a root,
Tumbled down in a silly suit.
The owl hooted, spied the show,
And kept a tally – funny, though!

Beneath the boughs, a party's found,
Where laughter echoes all around.
Join the fun, it's quite a treat,
In this woodland, none feel beat!

Breaths of the Birch

A birch tree quipped, 'I'm feeling fine!'
While snails slid down, one took a line.
They raced for glory, slipping fast,
But ended up in a puddle, at last!

Leaves whispered secrets, soft and sweet,
While bees buzzed in their tiny fleet.
A ladybug, on a dare,
Wore a hat that caused a stare!

Frogs croaked jokes, while toads croaked sighs,
Did you hear about the cat that flies?
They leaped and leered, with gleeful grins,
As crickets danced on their violin skins!

The sun peeked through, a golden beam,
And caught a spider in a dream.
With webs like lace, they spun about,
In this birch grove, laughter's what it's about!

Stories from the Stump

A wise old stump had tales to tell,
Of ants who'd danced and done quite well.
Each time they twirled, they'd drop their crumbs,
The fat raccoon chuckled at their bums!

A chipmunk slipped while chasing seeds,
And tangled up in viney weeds.
The owls hooted, so amused,
While the chipmunk groaned, oh so confused!

The hedgehog rolled, in dandelions,
Declaring war on the pesky lions.
But to their shock, they found them fake,
Just playful shadows, a laughing break!

So gather 'round the old stump now,
Listen closely, take a bow.
In this realm of laughs galore,
It's all in fun, forevermore!

Fables in the Forest Floor

A rabbit wrote a book of tricks,
How to leap and dodge those sticks.
But when it came to show it off,
He tripped on air and couldn't scoff!

A badger's dance could clear the way,
But no one knew the steps, they'd sway.
With paws all tangled, they created fun,
Even the stoic trees could run!

Some beetles formed a marching band,
But played their tunes just as they planned.
A frog croaked, "This is quite bizarre!"
And joined the tune with his guitar!

So if you tread this forest floor,
With space for laughter and much more.
The fables here keep spirits high,
With chuckles echoing toward the sky!

Stories Carved in the Core

In the forest deep, where the squirrels play,
A log once told of a very odd day.
The woodpecker laughed, with a tap-tap laugh,
While ants held a feast, a tiny snack craft.

A tree stump wore glasses, oh what a sight,
Reading old jokes by the soft moonlight.
The bark had its stories, the roots had their dreams,
In laughter and whispers, the forest redeems.

The chipmunks gathered, made a circus show,
With acorn hats, oh how they'd glow!
Each twist of a branch sparked a giggle or two,
As the trees leaned in to hear the hullabaloo.

So next time you stroll past a crooked old tree,
Remember the tales, and just let it be.
For every good log has a whimsy-filled heart,
In the woodsy world, it's a marvelous art.

The Pulse of Pine

In a patch of pines, where the owls hoot loud,
The needles giggle beneath a leafy shroud.
A squirrel named Simon, with acorns in tow,
Decided to hold a grand nut-counting show.

The pine cones applauded, a raucous cheer,
As Simon was counting, he suddenly veered.
He slipped on a pine cone, went flying in air,
Landed in laughter, without a care.

The boughs bent with giggles, like branches in glee,
As Simon exclaimed, "I'm just soaring, you see!"
The forest erupted, a chorus of fun,
In the heart of the pines, laughter's never done.

With every tall trunk, there's a heartbeat that sings,
A melody woven with magical strings.
So if you're out wandering, listen real close,
The pulse of the pine, is a funny old ghost.

Sapling Songs

Little saplings dance in a sunny glade,
With roots that wiggle, in a joyful parade.
They sing to the clouds, in a sweet, tiny voice,
While crickets strum softly, they all rejoice.

A breeze tickles leaves, they all sway and sway,
As the bunnies hop in, wanting to play.
They gather 'round close, for a hop and a spin,
With laughter and leaps, let the fun times begin!

Each droplet of dew, becomes glittering cheer,
Reflecting the sunshine, brightening the sphere.
The saplings all giggle, as they stretch up high,
Making friends with the butterflies that flit by.

So if you feel down, or you're stuck in a frown,
Find a patch of saplings, where joy wears a crown.
For in every small shoot, there's a song yet unsung,
In the heart of the forest, the laughter is flung.

Oak's Odyssey

Big old oak stood tall, with a gnarled old grin,
His branches a stage, where the critters begin.
With raccoons and rabbits, a wild little crew,
They planned out a party, a grand hullabaloo.

But the squirrels got crafty, with tricks up their sleeves,
They hung up the snacks, like autumnal leaves.
Each acorn was tied, with a twinkling string,
This party of laughter, oh what joy it would bring!

When the night finally came, and the moon hung low,
The oak held his breath, as the fun started to flow.
With dancing and singing, the forest alive,
Every critter mustered a giggle and thrive.

So remember dear friends, when you wander and roam,
That oak trees are full of a fun-loving home.
In their wise old embrace, there's a world yet to share,
With stories and laughter, floating sweet on the air.

www.ingramcontent.com/pod-product-compliance
Lightning Source LLC
Chambersburg PA
CBHW071827160426
43209CB00003B/217